CHICAGO PUBLIC LIBRARY
HEGEWISCH BRANCH
3048 E. 130TH ST.

FROM SEA to SHINING SEA

MINNESOTA

JUDY L. HASDAY

Consultants

MELISSA N. MATUSEVICH, PH.D.

Curriculum and Instruction Specialist
Blacksburg, Virginia

ENID COSTLEY, M.L.S.

Children's Librarian
Hibbing Public Library
Hibbing, Minnesota

JOYCE PETTINGER

Extension Services Supervisor and Children's Coordinator
Lake Agassiz Regional Library
Moorhead, Minnesota

CHILDREN'S PRESS®

A DIVISION OF SCHOLASTIC INC.

New York • Toronto • London • Auckland • Sydney • Mexico City
New Delhi • Hong Kong • Danbury, Connecticut

Minnesota is in the north central part of the United States. It is bordered by Wisconsin, Lake Superior, Iowa, South Dakota, North Dakota, Ontario, and Manitoba.

The photograph on the front cover shows an old farmhouse in rural Lincoln County.

Project Editor: Meredith DeSousa
Art Director: Marie O'Neill
Photo Researcher: Marybeth Kavanagh
Design: Robin West, Ox and Company, Inc.
Page 6 map and recipe art: Susan Hunt Yule
All other maps: XNR Productions, Inc.

Library of Congress Cataloging-in-Publication Data

Hasday, Judy L., 1957-
    Minnesota / Judy L. Hasday.
        p. cm. — (From sea to shining sea)
Summary: Takes the reader on a tour of the state called "The North Star State," emphasizing its geography, history, government, and culture.
Includes bibliographical references and index.
    ISBN 0-516-22478-6
    1. Minnesota—Juvenile literature. [1. Minnesota.] I. Title. II. Series.

F606.3 .H37 2003
977.6—dc21   2002001611

TABLE of CONTENTS

CHAPTER ONE

INTRODUCING THE NORTH STAR STATE

Minnesotans embrace the cold winters.

If you like being near water, you'll love Minnesota. In fact, the state is famous for having thousands of lakes—about 12,000 in total! Because of `this, one of Minnesota's nicknames is the Land of 10,000 Lakes. There are also hundreds of smaller bodies of water called ponds, adding up to more than 22,000 bodies of water within Minnesota. Even the state name refers to water. It is translated from the Dakota Indian word *minisota,* meaning "sky-tinted water."

Minnesota's official nickname is the North Star State because it lies farther north than any other state except Alaska. Thanks to its northern location, winters can be very cold. In fact, on many winter days, International Falls, Minnesota, records the lowest temperature in the continental United States.

What else comes to mind when you think of Minnesota?

- The headwaters of the mighty Mississippi River at Lake Itasca
- Canoes winding their way through Voyageurs National Park
- Waterskiing, which was invented in Minnesota on Lake Pepin in 1922
- The Minneapolis Sculpture Garden, the largest urban sculpture garden in the country
- Doctors taking care of patients at the world-renowned Mayo Clinic
- Freighters being loaded with ore, coal, and grain at the port of Duluth
- The country's largest shopping mall—the Mall of America in Bloomington
- Ice fishing on frozen lakes

Minnesota has a diverse landscape that includes lakes, grasslands, soil-rich farmland, and red pine timber forests. In this book, you'll read about the people and places that have contributed to the growth and development of the North Star State. You'll learn the story of Minnesota.

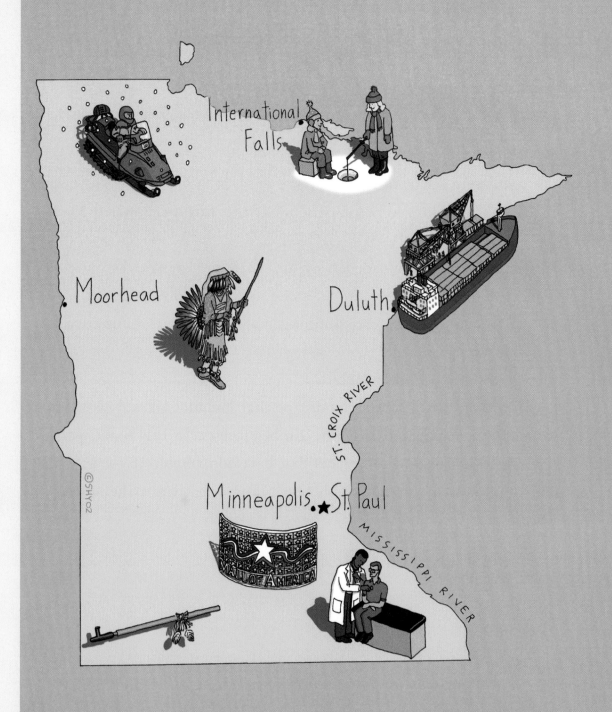

International Falls

Moorhead

Duluth

ST. CROIX RIVER

Minneapolis • ★ St. Paul

MALL OF AMERICA

MISSISSIPPI RIVER

©SHY02

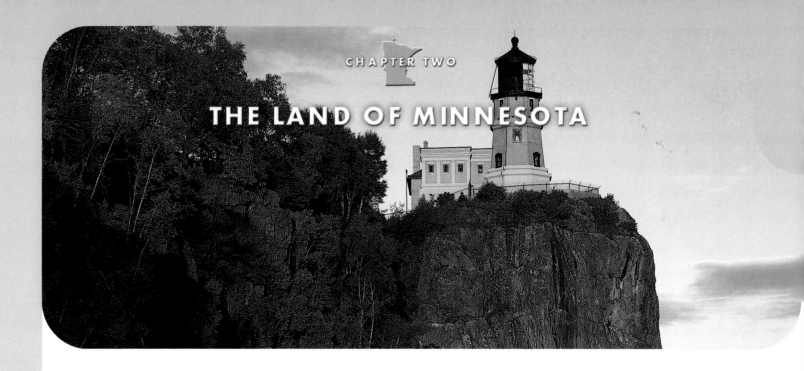

CHAPTER TWO

THE LAND OF MINNESOTA

Minnesota is located in the north central part of the United States. It is one of the largest states in this region, occupying about 86,943 square miles (225,181 square kilometers). If you traveled east to west across the state you would cover 357 miles (575 kilometers). North to south, Minnesota is about 411 miles (661 km). It is large enough that Connecticut, Delaware, Maryland, New Hampshire, Vermont, and Virginia would fit inside its borders, with room left over.

Minnesota resembles a rectangle with a piece taken out of the side by its eastern neighbor, Wisconsin. Minnesota's northern neighbors are Manitoba and Ontario, two provinces of another country, Canada. To the west lie North Dakota and South Dakota, and to the south is Iowa.

An arrowhead-shaped wedge of Minnesota lies above an important body of water along its northeastern border—Lake Superior, the largest

Split Rock Lighthouse, built in 1910, once kept watch over the waters of Lake Superior.

Depressions in the bedrock are found along the shore of Lake Superior at Grand Marais.

lake in North America. Lake Superior laps against more than 150 miles (241 km) of Minnesota's shoreline. In total area, it is the second largest lake in the world.

If you travel through Minnesota from north to south, you might feel as if you were passing through different states at different times of the year. That's because Minnesota has many land features and weather conditions. Some of its landscape is rocky and primitive; some is heavily

forested. Much of Minnesota's land is undeveloped. There are also miles of grassy plains, as well as fertile fields that are used for farming.

More than 16,000 years ago, during the Ice Age, huge glaciers moved across the land of Minnesota. (The Ice Age refers to a period of time when large areas of the Earth were covered with thick sheets of ice.) At one time, these ice formations were almost one mile (1.6 km) deep—five times thicker than the tallest skyscraper in Manhattan!

Glaciers moved and reshaped the land like a bulldozer. As they slid over land, the glaciers cut into it, leaving behind a gouged landscape of hills, ravines, and valleys. As the ice melted, the ravines filled with water,

Native prairie grasses are preserved in southwestern Minnesota at Blue Mounds State Park.

forming lakes of various sizes and shapes. After the ice melted, four geographic regions were created: the Superior Upland, the Young Drift Plains, the Dissected Till Plains, and the Driftless Area.

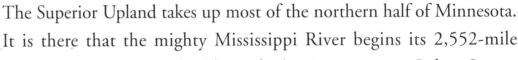

THE SUPERIOR UPLAND

The Superior Upland takes up most of the northern half of Minnesota. It is there that the mighty Mississippi River begins its 2,552-mile (4,107-km) journey at Lake Itasca. Although the Mississippi River is the largest river in the United States, it begins as a small stream about 10 feet (3 meters) wide and 2 feet (.6 m) deep at Lake Itasca.

The glaciers had little effect on this region. The Superior Upland is rugged and undeveloped. Large rock formations and boulders are common. Much of Minnesota's iron ore deposits are found in the Superior Upland. The Mesabi (an Ojibwe word for "giant") Range has a section of iron ore 110 miles (177 km) long, 1 to 3 miles (1.6 to 5 km) wide, and reaching a thickness as great as 500 feet (152 m).

Minnesota's one national park, Voyageurs, is located in this region. The

Huge open-pit mines are located throughout the Mesabi Range.

park is unique because it has no roads. To get there you must travel on water, either frozen or liquid, as fur traders did in the 1700s and 1800s. The park offers fun and recreation in summer and winter.

One of the most remote parts of the Superior Upland region is Arrowhead County. If you look at a map of the state, this part of Minnesota looks like the shape of an arrowhead. The highest point in the state, Eagle Mountain, is in this region. It stands 2,301 feet (701 m) high—almost half a mile. Minnesotans travel to this part of the state to canoe, ski, hike, snowmobile, and engage in other activities because of its true wilderness feel. Among the lakes and

With more than 80,000 acres (32,375 hectares) of water, Voyageurs National Park is a boater's paradise.

FIND OUT MORE

Iron ore is an important mineral resource. Many things are made from it, including steel, ships, bridges, and cars. What other things can be made from iron ore?

forested areas you can hear the howl of Minnesota timber-wolves, gray fur-covered wild animals that look like large dogs.

THE YOUNG DRIFT PLAINS

Vastly different from the Superior Upland, the Young Drift Plains area begins with the fertile Red River Valley at the state's northwestern border. It extends through the central and south central parts of Minnesota. Glaciers that moved across this region smoothed the land flat. As the glaciers continued to melt, they left behind fertile topsoil called drift. As a result, the best farmland in the state is found in the Young Drift Plains. It is not unusual for farmers in this region to harvest more crops than in other parts of the nation.

Only a small number of timberwolves (also called gray wolves) live in the wild in the continental United States.

The young drift plains in southwestern Minnesota consists of low, rolling farmland.

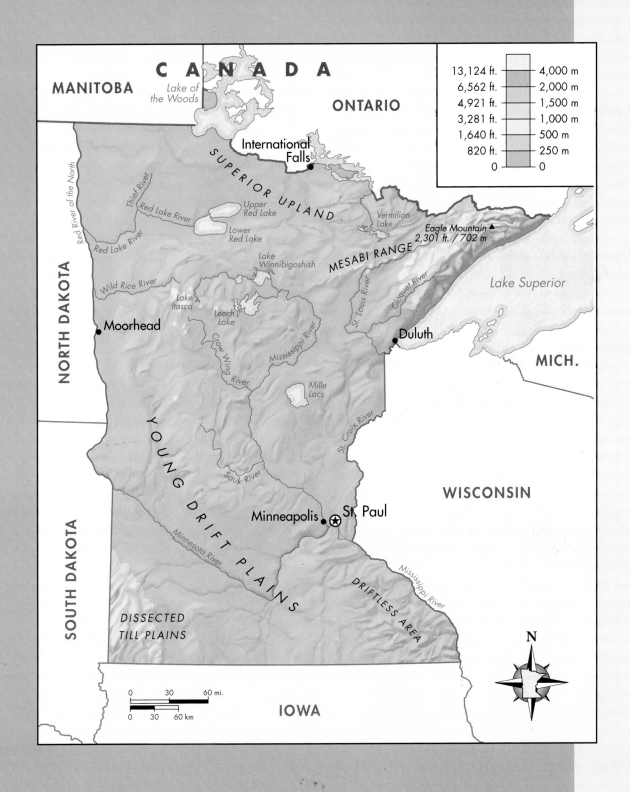

MANITOBA

CANADA

Lake of
the Woods

ONTARIO

International
Falls

SUPERIOR UPLAND

Red River of the North

Thief River

Red Lake River

Upper
Red Lake

Vermilion
Lake

Eagle Mountain ▲
2,301 ft. / 702 m

NORTH DAKOTA

Red Lake River

Lower
Red Lake

Lake
Winnibigoshish

MESABI RANGE

Wild Rice River

Lake
Itasca

Leech
Lake

Crow Wing River

Mississippi River

St. Louis River

Cloquet River

Lake Superior

Moorhead

Duluth

MICH.

Mille
Lacs

YOUNG DRIFT PLAINS

St. Croix River

WISCONSIN

Sauk River

Minneapolis ●⊛ St. Paul

Minnesota River

DRIFTLESS AREA

Mississippi River

SOUTH DAKOTA

DISSECTED
TILL PLAINS

N

0   30   60 mi.

0   30   60 km

IOWA

13,124 ft.   4,000 m
6,562 ft.   2,000 m
4,921 ft.   1,500 m
3,281 ft.   1,000 m
1,640 ft.   500 m
820 ft.   250 m
0   0

THE DISSECTED TILL PLAINS

This small region is found in the southwestern corner of Minnesota. As glaciers moved over this area, they left behind a mixture of sand, gravel, and clay soil material called till. Small rivers and streams have dissected or cut up the land.

At one time, herds of buffalo roamed the grassy plains of this region. The Dakota Indians settled there because they depended on buffalo for food and other supplies.

THE DRIFTLESS AREA

The Driftless Area is a small section along the Mississippi River in the southeastern corner of the state. It got its name because the glaciers never moved over this region. Aside from the Superior Upland, the Driftless Area has some of the most rugged terrain in the state.

Limestone hills made from shells and coral border the river valleys, where many caves and fast-flowing trout streams are found. Hardwood trees such as the black walnut and red mulberry thrive in the warm temperatures and moderate rainfall. The Driftless Area is also home to more reptiles and amphibians than any other part of the state. The only two poisonous snakes in Minnesota can be found there. They are the common timber rattlesnake and the massasauga (Ojibwe for "great river-mouth"), a rare poisonous rattlesnake. The massasauga gets its name because it prefers to be near water and is often found around the mouths of rivers.

More than 6,564 rivers flow through Minnesota. Together with its lakes, Minnesota has 90,000 miles (144,841 km) of shoreline—more than California, Florida, and Hawaii combined.

The state's largest lake, found in the northwestern part of Minnesota, is Red Lake. It covers 432 square miles (1,119 sq km). Other large lakes in the region include Lake of the Woods, Leech Lake, Winnibigoshish Lake, and Vermilion Lake. Large lakes in other parts of Minnesota include Big Stone Lake, Mille Lacs Lake, and Lake Minnetonka.

The mighty Mississippi River begins its journey southward from Lake Itasca in the north-central part of Minnesota. The Mississippi creates a natural border in the southeast with neighboring Wisconsin. Several rivers branch off of the Mississippi, including the Minnesota, Crow Wing, St. Croix, and Sauk rivers. In the northwest, the Red River forms the border with North Dakota.

Friends enjoy a lazy summer day fishing on Mille Lacs Lake.

All this water has helped create beautiful waterfalls. Poet Henry Wadsworth Longfellow made the 50-foot (15.2-m) Minnehaha Falls famous in his poem *The Song of Hiawatha*. The 49-foot (15-m) Falls of St. Anthony, located along the Mississippi River, was used as an important source of electric power when Minneapolis was being developed. Minnesota's highest waterfall,

Although it is surrounded by natural scenic beauty, Minnehaha Falls is located in the heart of Minneapolis.

Cascade Falls, tumbles down 124 feet (38 m)—about as high as an eight-story building.

CLIMATE

Minnesotans will be first to tell you that Minnesota gets very cold. In fact, they have described their climate as having six months of winter and six months of tough sledding. In the Minneapolis-St. Paul area, the temperature drops below 0° Fahrenheit (−18° Celsius) about thirty to thirty-five days a year. International Falls, which often records the coldest temperatures in the nation, is likely to have below 0° F readings about 70 days per year.

Minnesotans embrace their long, intense winters. They play outside in winter just as actively as they do in summer. Instead of waterskiing in a tranquil lake, they snowmobile across its thick ice covering. With more than 15,000 miles (24,140 km) of maintained trails, it is no surprise that one in twenty Minnesotans owns a snowmobile.

Minnesotans enjoy the cold weather—and giant ice slides—at the annual winter carnival in St. Paul.

Serious fishermen don't let the cold and ice prevent them from participating in their favorite pastime. In winter they ice fish by setting up a heated "fish house," cutting a hole in the ice, and dropping in a fishing line.

Summer temperatures in Minnesota usually hover around the low-to mid-70s F (20s C). Minnesotans spend their summers outdoors, too. There are plenty of lakes for the population's avid boaters. About one in six Minnesotans owns a boat.

Yearly precipitation (rain, sleet, and snow) varies by region. Northern cities such as Duluth and International Falls have the highest averages of rain and snow in the state. It is not unusual for Duluth to have 80 inches (203 centimeters) of snow in one winter season.

Cities such as Moorhead and Windom in western and southern Minnesota have the least amount of wet weather. However, sometimes spring brings lots of rain just as winter's snow and ice begins to thaw, and some rivers swell to overflowing. As a result, water sometimes floods cities, towns, and farmland nearest the riverbanks.

Droughts, or long periods without rain, can cause serious problems as well. During the nationwide drought of 1988, many Minnesota farmers lost hundreds of acres of crops. Water was so scarce that even the famous cascading Minnehaha Falls dried up.

CHAPTER THREE

MINNESOTA THROUGH HISTORY

People have lived in the land we call Minnesota for more than 10,000 years. Archaeologists—people who study relics and artifacts of past civilizations—have discovered ancient skeletons, pieces of pottery, copper tools, arrowheads, and jewelry. Old drawings on rocks and walls of caves, called petroglyphs, portray people, animals, and other symbols. These drawings give us a clue as to what Minnesota's early people were like.

Geologists believe that early people called Paleo-Indians were nomads (people who move from one place to another in search of food). They inhabited the Americas at the end of the Ice Age, a time when the earth was covered with thick sheets of ice called glaciers. They followed herds of

Early Native Americans in Minnesota carved images into rock, called petroglyphs. The petroglyphs shown here are found at Pipestone National Monument.

FIND OUT MORE

In 1932, a construction crew uncovered a woman's skeleton believed to be 8,000 years old. Although she was a woman, she came to be known as "Minnesota Man." How do you think her world differed from yours? How did she travel? What did she eat? Where did she live? What might have been her hobbies?

large animals, such as mammoths (huge animals bigger than elephants) and bison, which they hunted for food. As the glaciers continued to melt and the land thawed, other foods such as fruits, berries, and nuts became available.

About 6,000 years ago, seminomadic people (people who moved with the seasons) living near Lake Superior discovered copper—a soft, reddish metal. They pounded the copper into knives and spear points. These people were probably among the first in the world to make metal tools.

About 2,500 years ago, Woodland people (early Native Americans) in this region set up permanent villages. They began making pottery from clay, and built earthen burial mounds. They harvested and stored rice. They began using bows and arrows instead of spears.

During this time, the Woodland people built thousands of large earthen mounds. Although the mounds rise only four or five feet (1.2 or 1.5 m), some were more than 50 feet (15 m) around. The mounds were built to mark where chieftans and other important tribe members were buried. They were also used as places of worship. Some were made in the shapes of birds, buffalo, or snakes; others were adorned with jewelry and per-

This photo of a prehistoric mound was taken at Mound Park in 1900.

sonal belongings. Only a small number of mounds remain today.

Descendants of the Woodland people, called the Mississippians, wandered south of Lake Superior to fertile prairie land. Still other groups wandered farther south. Archaeologists have found artifacts and agricultural tools in the southwestern and southeastern parts of Minnesota that are about 1,000 years old.

No one is sure what happened to these early natives. Although these people were rich in culture, traditions, and sophistication, they did not write, so there is no recorded history to study.

FIND OUT MORE

You can still see burial mounds in several places in Minnesota. One of these places is Indian Mounds Park, which sits on a bluff above the Mississippi River. From the park you can get a spectacular view of St. Paul and the river. Where else in Minnesota can you find burial mounds?

Early Native Americans hunted deer for food, clothing, and shelter.

NATIVE AMERICAN SETTLEMENTS

About 100 years before the arrival of European explorers, a group of Native Americans known as the Dakota (or Sioux) began to settle in small communities near Lake Superior, where the ground was fertile and water was readily available. They began picking berries and nuts for food. The Dakotas planted and harvested corn and other vegetable crops. They also migrated to the southwestern part of Minnesota and

settled in a region called Pipestone, where they mined a soft pinkish stone called catlinite. Five hundred years ago catlinite was plentiful. The Dakota used it to carve ceremonial smoking pipes.

Other tribes occupied various parts of land that later became Minnesota. The Cheyenne occupied the area along the western edge; the Assinboin lived in the forested areas in the northwest; the Cree also lived up north near Lake Superior; and the Fox occupied territory to the east near the St. Croix River. Despite the presence of these tribes, the Dakota dominated the region.

Native American men fished and hunted buffalo, deer, and elk in spring and summer. The women dried the meat to eat in winter, when animal herds were hard to find. They also used the dried animal skins to make clothing. In summer they lived in homes built from bark and wooden poles made from tree branches. Needing warmth in winter, they covered the poles with large dried animal hides.

In the 1600s, the Ojibwe (also known as the Chippewa), a rival tribe of the Dakota, began moving eastward from the St. Lawrence River toward the Great Lakes. They came to that part of Minnesota around the same time the first European explorers began arriving on the shores of Lake Superior.

THE FIRST EUROPEANS

In the 1500s, European explorers from France, England, and Spain began arriving in North America. Foreigners sought to claim territory (land) in the New World for their own countries. These European countries competed with each other to become rich and powerful. One way to do this was to acquire more land.

French explorers Pierre Espirit Radisson and Mèdard Chouart, Sieur des Groseilliers were among the first Europeans to visit Minnesota and to make contact with the Dakota. They explored along the shores of Lake Superior around 1656, and later returned to Montreal, Canada, with a bounty of animal furs. This was the start of the fur trade in the Great Lakes-Minnesota region.

Fur trappers were attracted to Minnesota because the area was rich in fur-bearing animals.

The explorers traded weapons and other goods with Native Americans in exchange for furs. Small animal furs were very valuable to the explorers. Back home in their own countries, the furs were made into hats and coats. The demand for furs forced many Native Americans to find new trapping territories, as they began compete with each other for trading rights with the foreigners.

In 1678, Frenchman Daniel Greysolon, Sieur Du Luth set out from Montreal, Canada, to explore the area around Lake Superior. A year later, he met Dakota tribe members in the city that now bears his name (Duluth). The Dakota were friendly, and Greysolon followed them to one of their villages near present-day Mille Lacs, in central

Minnesota. He claimed the region for the king of France, Louis XIV. Sponsored by merchants in Canada, Greysolon wanted to establish fur trading with the Dakota. He also traded with several other tribes, including the Ojibwe.

Other European explorers sought to bring the Christian religion to Native Americans. In 1680 a missionary, or priest, from Belgium, Father Louis Hennepin, came to Minnesota to spread Christianity. The Dakota didn't know how to interact with him and his two companions, so they took the three men prisoner. Daniel Greysolon later arranged for Father Hennepin's release.

Hennepin made an important contribution to Minnesota's history by naming a waterfall he spotted while being taken to the Dakota camp. He named it the Falls of St. Anthony. Father Hennepin's name also lives on in several streets and parks in Minnesota.

Father Hennepin came to Minnesota to spread the Christian religion to Native Americans.

Like other countries, the British (English) also came to the New World in search of wealth. Both the British and the French wanted to dominate the fur trade, and in 1754 war broke out between the two countries. The Seven Years' War (also called the French and Indian War, 1754–1763) took place in the Great Lakes region. Many Native Americans sided with the French, because they felt that British traders were unfriendly and disrespectful. Despite this, however, the war ended in victory for the British in 1763. Britain immediately laid claim to all French territories in North America, including parts of present-day Canada and Minnesota.

The British established trading companies all along the Great Lakes. These companies made money by trading furs and other goods. Two of the largest were the Hudson Bay Company and the North West Company.

WHAT'S IN A NAME?

Many names of Minnesota places have interesting origins.

Name	Comes From or Means
Anoka	A combination of the Dakota word *A-no-ka-tan-han*, meaning "on both sides of the river," and the Ojibwe word *On-o-kay*, meaning "working waters"
Dakota	Dakota (Sioux) word for "friend"
Minnetonka	Dakota and Ojibwe for "big water"
Le Sueur	From the name of French explorer Pierre Charles Le Sueur
Minnehaha	Native American for "laughing water"
Minneapolis	A combination of the Dakota word *minne* for "water" and Greek *polis* for "city"

A NEW COUNTRY IS BORN

Up until this time, although they lived in America, British colonists in the East were still citizens of England and had to abide by the laws set forth by the king. By 1775, the colonists no longer wanted to be under English rule. Shortly after, they declared their independence from Great Britain, and went to war. The colonists won the Revolutionary War in 1783, and they established a new nation called the United States. Eastern Minnesota, which had been British territory, was given to the United States.

Western Minnesota followed in 1803, when France sold a vast area of land to the United States in what was called the Louisiana Purchase. The area covered 828,000 square miles (2,144,510 sq km) of land from the Mississippi River to the Rocky Mountains, and from the Gulf of Mexico to the Canadian border. The new territory doubled the size of the United States and included western Minnesota.

Lieutenant Zebulon Pike explored much of the western United States after the Louisiana Purchase.

A DEVELOPING LAND

In 1805, Lieutenant Zebulon Pike was sent to the Louisiana Territory. As an officer of the United States, Pike was to do three things: look for the headwaters of the Mississippi, negotiate peace treaties with Native Americans, and make legal claim to the area. In the northern part of the territory, where the Mississippi and Minnesota Rivers join, Pike signed a treaty for land with the Dakota tribe. He bought 155,520 acres (62,937 hectares) of Upper Mississippi land and water for $200 worth of presents and 60 gallons of whiskey. The treaty also granted the United States permission to build military posts. The United States army completed Fort Snelling (originally called Fort St. Anthony) in

1825. The fort was the site of the first school, hospital, and post office in the area.

Minnesota grew rapidly. The Mississippi River provided loggers with a means to transport lumber downriver to settled areas that became St. Paul and Minneapolis. Just north of Fort Snelling, settlers began using the waterpower of the Falls of St. Anthony to create electricity to run sawmills. The first commercial (large-scale) flourmill in the country was also built there, and a busy community developed nearby. The town of St. Anthony later became part of Minneapolis.

The building of Fort Snelling changed the landscape of Minnesota, adding roads, mills, and farming areas.

South of the falls was another small community known as Pig's Eye Landing. This town marked the northernmost point where a steamboat could safely travel on the Mississippi. Beyond that, the river was too shallow for a ship to navigate. Seeing a steamboat was an exciting event. Townspeople often gathered at the dock to see who was arriving and to find out what was going on in the rest of the country. Pig's Eye Landing later became St. Paul, the capital of Minnesota.

THE MINNESOTA TERRITORY

In 1849, Congress officially made Minnesota a territory, although there were fewer than 5,000 residents. With news of plentiful forests in the north and fertile plains in southern and western Minnesota, the territory expanded rapidly. As more people moved into the Minnesota Territory, shop merchants set up stores to handle the booming business.

With the influx of so many settlers, there was less open land available for wild animals to roam and Native Americans to live on. Soon, buffalo and other animal populations dwindled, and the Dakota and Ojibwe had difficulty finding food. At the same time, the United States government wanted more land. They forced the Indians to sign treaties, turning over large sections of their land to the government. By the mid-1800s, the Dakota and Ojibwe had sold most of their land in the Minnesota Territory, leaving them very small

The Dakotas were pushed off their land and forced onto small reservations.

areas on which to live. These areas of land, called reservations, were allocated to Native Americans by the United States government.

In the 1860s, an influx of new settlers came from European countries, including Germany, Sweden, Finland, Norway, Ireland, and the Ukraine, to work as lumberjacks and farmers. They came to America in the hope of improving their way of life.

Although there was plenty of land, farming was difficult on the prairies. Farmers endured blistering heat in the summer and bitter cold in winter. Droughts, floods, snowstorms, and insect plagues were common. Only a few schools existed, and most children had to work on their parents' farms instead of attending school.

Farmwork was exhausting. The land had to be plowed, and the crops harvested. Farm animals had to be fed, cows milked, and chickens' eggs

This drawing shows Minneapolis in the 1880s.

collected. Women cleaned clothes and linens, cooked meals, canned and dried food, and made items such as butter, soap, and candles. Despite the exhausting work, the opportunity to farm one's own land was very appealing.

By 1855, settlers living in the Minnesota Territory greatly outnumbered the fewer than 20,000 Native Americans who remained. With a population well over the 60,000 settlers required to join the Union, Minnesota was granted statehood on May 11, 1858. It was the thirty-second state. By then, 150,000 people lived there—twenty-five times the population eight years earlier.

FIRST TO FIGHT

In the late 1850s and early 1860s, people of the United States became involved in a great controversy. It began back in the 1600s, when Dutch settlers sailed to the shores of America and brought African people with them. The Dutch had kidnapped these people from their homes on the African coast. In America, the Africans were forced to perform hard labor on farms. The Africans, called slaves, were often traded for things like molasses, sugar, and rum.

By the 1700s, slave trading was common in towns up and down the Atlantic Coast, particularly in the South. As America continued to grow, large farms called plantations were established in southern states such as Virginia, North Carolina, South Carolina, Mississippi, and Georgia, where tobacco and cotton grew well in the warm climate. Harvesting the crops was hard work and required a lot of people. Slaves were particularly useful because they weren't paid for their labor.

Most people in the North felt that slavery was wrong, and many others thought it should be abolished, or done away with. The northern states were called free states, where slavery was not allowed. Southerners felt threatened by this. They feared that the United States government would try to end slavery.

Minnesota was a free state. However, the towns of St. Anthony and Minneapolis along the Mississippi River were favorite summer vacation spots for southern slave owners. Minnesotans were conflicted: they opposed slavery but did not feel they should become involved in the business of others.

Debate about the slavery issue continued for many years. In 1861, to protect their rights, the southern states seceded

WHO'S WHO IN MINNESOTA?

Dred Scott (c. 1799–1858) was the most famous slave to enter Minnesota. He belonged to Dr. John Emerson, a United States Army officer in Missouri (a slave state). When Emerson was assigned to duty at Fort Snelling, he brought Scott with him. Scott later returned to Missouri with his master. When Emerson died, Scott believed that he should be a free man because he had once lived in a territory that banned slavery. In 1846 he filed a lawsuit against Emerson's wife. Scott's case was debated in many courts until 1857, when the United States Supreme Court made the final ruling: as a slave Scott was not a citizen, and therefore he had no rights. The Dred Scott case was one of the most important cases ever tried in the United States.

(withdrew) from the Union and established their own government. They called themselves the Confederate States of America. It wasn't long before the Civil War (1861–1865) broke out between North and South. Minnesota's governor offered to send 1,000 soldiers to fight against the Confederacy. These troops were the first volunteer soldiers for the Union.

Although no battles were fought on Minnesota soil, about 25,000 Minnesota men fought in the war. Almost 2,500 of them died. Many Minnesota soldiers fought in one of the most important battles of the war in Gettysburg, Pennsylvania. There, in July 1863, the 1st Minnesota Volunteer Infantry Regiment fought bravely alongside other famous regiments, such as the 20th Maine and the 140th New York. The 1st Minnesota played a key role in winning the battle, where 9 in every 10 of its soldiers lost their lives.

The 1st Minnesota Regiment is best known for its dramatic charge at the Battle of Gettysburg.

THE DAKOTA CONFLICT

While the Civil War raged, more trouble arose in Minnesota. After selling most of their land to the government, the Dakota tribe had been relocated onto a 10-mile (16-km) strip of land along the Minnesota River. The United States government promised the Dakotas money and food in exchange for leaving their land, but the government didn't deliver. Because hunting was poor and crops were destroyed by pests, the Dakotas went hungry. Settlers refused to trade goods with the Dakota or give them food because they felt it was the government's responsibility. Meanwhile, the Dakotas were starving to death. This ill treatment by the "white man" fueled the Dakota's anger.

Some members of the tribe decided to reclaim their land. In 1862 the Dakota raided farms in 23 counties, burning buildings and killing entire families. After a few weeks they were defeated by a group of civilians and military units. Nearly 600 settlers, soldiers, and Native Americans died in the conflict. Today, a memorial to those who died is located at Reconciliation Park in Markato.

The Dakota rebels were captured and brought to trial. Thirty-eight were charged with murder and hanged in December 1862. Hundreds more were imprisoned. The tribe's reservation was taken away, and the remaining occupants were driven into a barren area of South Dakota. Many died there of starvation or disease. Very few Dakota, who once lived in abundance and hunted the lands freely, remained in Minnesota.

WHO'S WHO IN MINNESOTA?

Little Crow Ta-oyate-duta (c. 1820–1863) (Dakota for "his red people") was named by white settlers. He was a brave and ambitious leader of the Dakota Indians. When men of his tribe decided to attack white settlers in 1862, they asked Little Crow to lead the campaign. He escaped Minnesota Territory after the uprising, but he was captured and killed in 1863.

The United States government needed a way to dispose of the public land it had acquired. In 1862 the government passed the Homestead Act, which promised 160 free acres (65 ha) in Minnesota and other western territories to anyone willing to live on the land and farm it. At the end of five years, the land would become the property of the caretaker if they built a house on it and plowed 10 acres (4 ha). Thousands of Americans and European immigrants took advantage of the deal.

Construction of the state's first rail line, the Minnesota & Pacific Railroad, began soon after. It linked the towns of St. Paul and St. Anthony. Later, it became part of the Great Northern Railway, which stretched to the Pacific Ocean. The railroad system helped move people and goods to their destinations more quickly than by boat or wagon.

The Northern Pacific railroad crossed the Mississippi River at Brainerd.

Farmers paid high prices to railroad owners to have their products shipped east. They were charged another high fee for storing their crops in tall structures called grain elevators. Farm families lost still more money when milling companies bought wheat for low prices. As a result, farmers made very little, if any, profit. To change this unfair system, farmers banded together and formed cooperatives. This allowed them to negotiate better shipping rates from the railroads. By pooling their money, they could also purchase their own grain elevators, mills, and farm equipment to share among the cooperative's members.

In 1867, a Minnesota farmer named Oliver Kelley founded a cooperative called the Grange. This powerful group created an organization across the United States to protect the rights of small farmers. It helped set limits on railroad shipping charges and encouraged farmers across the country to share new methods of farming.

THE LOGGING INDUSTRY

Before settlers arrived, much of Minnesota was forested. With so much potential wood available, loggers came to the region and cut down millions of trees. Lumberjacks sent the logs downstream, each marked with a company symbol. The logs arrived at mills where they were made into boards. So many logs were sent at once that rivers often became completely jammed.

Logging created thousands of jobs for Minnesota settlers, but in the rush to mill as much lumber as possible, the companies destroyed entire

Loggers transported huge loads of lumber from Minnesota's thick forests.

forests. None of the trees were replaced. Loggers often left only stumps behind. With little forested area left in northern Minnesota by the early 1900s, one-third of the state was treeless.

MINING IN MINNESOTA

In the late 1800s, a man named Lewis Merritt unsuccessfully prospected (searched) for iron ore on the Minnesota mountain ridge known as the Mesabi. Iron ore could be converted into steel, so it was a valuable resource. After his death, Merritt's seven sons continued to search for ore. In 1890, they found what they were looking for.

Prospectors flocked to the Mesabi Range and to two other nearby ranges: the Vermilion and the Cuyuna. Minnesota soon became the nation's largest source of ore. Quiet communities in the northeastern part of the state, such as Hibbing, Ironton, Babbitt, and Chisholm, became bustling towns. People moved to the region to mine or to set up businesses to supply townspeople with food and other goods and services. Between 1890 and 1920, a new wave of immigrants arrived from Italy, Hungary, Poland, and the former Yugoslavia to work as miners.

The most important city for the transportation of iron ore was Duluth, located on Lake Superior. From Duluth's port, the state shipped 12 million tons (11 million metric tons) of ore each year. Most of it was sent to steel mills in Pennsylvania.

EXTRA! EXTRA!

In 1889, Captain Alexander McDougall devised a ship called the "whaleback" steamer, named after its rounded deck and flat bottom. Whalebacks were faster than other steamships, so they transported grain and iron ore more economically than other ships. McDougall built more than 40 whalebacks in Duluth, which became known as an important center for building cargo ships. His sturdily designed vessels transported iron ore until the 1930s.

TWO WORLD WARS

As America grew and prospered, life was tense in Europe. Several powerful countries, including Germany and Austria-Hungary, entered into military agreements and went to war with England, France, and other European countries.

When World War I (1914–1918) broke out, Minnesota's wheat and iron ore were in great demand overseas. There was a great need for food to feed soldiers abroad and citizens at home, and steel was needed to

Many women began to work in Minnesota factories for the first time during World War I.

make weapons and war machinery. After the United States entered World War I in 1917, the state's industries helped feed, clothe, and arm thousands of American soldiers. Minnesota sent close to 120,000 soldiers and 1,000 nurses to serve in World War I.

After the war ended in 1918, the United States continued to enjoy success in trade and industry. Milk production and the construction of new banks and office buildings were among the fastest-growing businesses in Minnesota. Signs of trouble were on the horizon, however.

In 1929, a period of enormous financial difficulty known as the Great Depression set in around the country. Too many products were being produced, and not enough people had money to buy them. One-third of factory workers in Minneapolis and St. Paul were laid off because companies did not have the money to pay them. In Minnesota, 7 in 10 miners had lost their jobs by 1932. Many farmers lost everything as wheat and dairy prices plummeted. Throughout the country, long lines of people waited outside soup kitchens, where charitable organizations handed out free food.

The Great Depression gradually came to an end around 1941, during World War II (1939–1945). The war in Europe broke out after Germany invaded neighboring Poland. In the Pacific, Japan was expanding its territory, too. The Japanese invaded China and were looking toward Pearl Harbor, on the Hawaiian island of Oahu where the United States Pacific Naval Fleet was stationed. On December 7, 1941, the Japanese carried out a sneak attack on Pearl Harbor, bombing warships and airfields. More than 2,000 sailors died in the attack.

America declared war on Japan the next day, officially entering World War II in December 1941. As America again prepared for battle, Minnesota's iron mines, factories, and farms produced guns, ammunition, uniforms, and food for the war effort. Of the 300,000 Minnesotans who joined the armed forces, 6,000 died serving their country. Even Governor Harold Stassen left his job to serve in the army overseas.

POSTWAR MINNESOTA

The 1940s and 1950s brought great growth and change to Minnesota. After the war, Minnesota began building new highways, bridges, river dams, airports, and hospitals. In the 1950s, census records showed that many Minnesotans left rural areas for cities and suburbs. This was a big change from a few decades earlier, when about 90 in 100 residents lived on farms.

By the 1950s, many of Minnesota's iron ore sites were depleted, or used up, and several mines were closed. They later reopened to mine taconite, a lower-quality grade of ore. In 1959 the St. Lawrence Seaway opened. This enabled freight ships to sail from the port of Duluth to ports around the world.

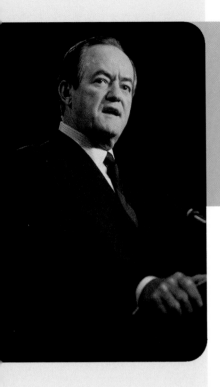

MODERN TIMES

In recent years, some Minnesotans accepted important positions in the national spotlight. Former governor Orville Freeman became secretary of agriculture under President John F. Kennedy. Distinguished senator Hubert H. Humphrey was elected vice president of the United States in 1964. St. Paul native Warren Burger became chief justice of the United States Supreme Court in 1969, and Harry Blackmun of Rochester was appointed to the Court in 1970.

In 1968, Native Americans from Minnesota tackled issues of national importance. Frustrated and angry at the way they were being treated, more than 200 members of the Indian community met to discuss problems such as poor living conditions and high unemployment. As a result, they formed an organization called AIM (American Indian Movement). In 1973, the Minnesota Dakota joined other Native Americans in taking over the town of Wounded Knee, South Dakota, to protest the government's ill treatment of Native Americans. The takeover turned into a violent siege. Two people were killed and several were injured. AIM leaders were arrested but not convicted of any crimes.

In the 1970s, environmental concerns became important in Minnesota. Taconite mines had severely polluted the water and air. One of the biggest offenders was the Reserve Mining Company of Silver Bay, which dumped huge amounts of chemical waste into Lake Superior. Traces of the chemicals were linked to cancer and appeared in Duluth's drinking water. In 1978 the Minnesota Supreme Court ordered the company to stop dumping in the lake. The company opened a waste-disposal site on its own land in 1980.

Polluted water from an iron mining plant pours into Lake Superior.

Minnesota's political "personality" has always been unique. Minnesotans are known to be independent thinkers. In 1998, Minnesota voters surprised the rest of the country by electing former professional wrestler Jesse "the Body" Ventura to be governor. Since then, he has helped to improve the quality of life for its citizens.

WHO'S WHO IN MINNESOTA?

Jesse Ventura (1951–), born James Janos, is a former professional wrestler. He was elected the 38th governor of Minnesota on November 3, 1998. Ventura was born in Minneapolis.

CHAPTER FOUR

GOVERNING MINNESOTA

The capitol building is the center of Minnesota's government.

Minnesotans have always been independent thinkers and innovators. Nowhere is this more apparent than in their government. Quite often Minnesota has been a leader in making improvements to education, business and industry, and the environment.

The citizens of Minnesota are governed by their constitution. Within the constitution, the state's basic principles and laws are outlined, defining how its elected officials will govern. Although the Minnesota constitution was adopted in 1857, it is never final. Since then, more than one hundred amendments (changes) have been approved by its citizens during regular or special elections.

Minnesota's government is set up the same way as our nation's government. There are three parts, called branches: the executive, legislative, and judicial. All three branches work together to serve the citizens and protect their rights under the law.

EXECUTIVE BRANCH

The job of the executive branch is to enforce Minnesota laws. The governor is head of the executive branch. He or she is elected by the people. The governor serves a four-year term and may be re-elected to serve any number of times.

The governor has the power to sign laws passed by the legislature (Minnesota's lawmaking body) or block laws with a veto (the power to reject a proposed law). Many people in the governor's administration help carry out the responsibilities of the executive branch. Those people include the lieutenant governor, secretary of state, attorney general, treasurer, and auditor.

Inside the capitol, law-makers meet in the legislative chambers to discuss new laws.

LEGISLATIVE BRANCH

The legislative branch introduces and passes laws. For example, the legislature recently passed a law that provides money to make sure all children eat breakfast each schoolday. The legislators also set the amount citizens are taxed. This is how funds are raised to pay for public services such as paving or repairing roads. One of the most important jobs of the legislative branch is to create a budget—a written statement of how money is to be spent—to pay for services statewide.

Minnesota's legislature has two parts, called houses: the senate and the house of representatives. There are

MINNESOTA GOVERNORS

Name	Term	Name	Term
Henry H. Sibley	1858–1860	Jacob A.O. Preus	1921–1925
Alexander Ramsey	1860–1863	Theodore Christianson	1925–1931
Henry Swift	1863–1864	Floyd B. Olson	1931–1936
Stephen Miller	1864–1866	Hjalmar Petersen	1936–1937
William R. Marshall	1866–1870	Elmer A. Benson	1937–1939
Horace Austin	1870–1874	Harold E. Stassen	1939–1943
Cushman K. Davis	1874–1876	Edward J. Thye	1943–1947
John S. Pillsbury	1876–1882	Luther W. Youngdahl	1947–1951
Lucius F. Hubbard	1882–1887	C. Elmer Anderson	1951–1955
Andrew R. McGill	1887–1889	Orville L. Freeman	1955–1961
William R. Merriam	1889–1893	Elmer Anderson	1961–1963
Knute Nelson	1893–1895	Karl F. Rolvaag	1963–1967
David M. Clough	1895–1899	Harold E. LeVander	1967–1971
John Lind	1899–1901	Wendell R. Anderson	1971–1976
Samuel R. Van Sant	1901–1905	Rudolph G. Perpich	1976–1979
John A. Johnson	1905–1909	Albert H. Quie	1979–1983
Adolph O. Eberhart	1909–1915	Rudolph G. Perpich	1983–1991
Winfield S. Hammond	1915	Arne H. Carlson	1991–1999
Joseph A. A. Burnquist	1915–1921	James G. Janos (Jesse Ventura)	1999–

MINNESOTA STATE GOVERNMENT

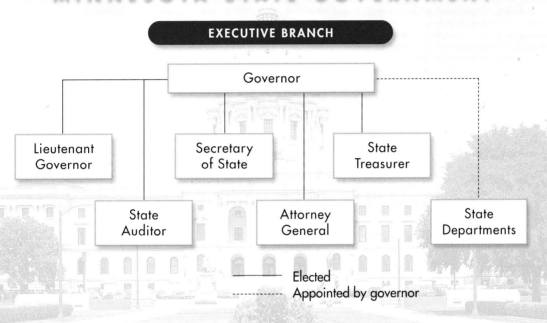

EXECUTIVE BRANCH

Governor

Lieutenant Governor

Secretary of State

State Treasurer

State Auditor

Attorney General

State Departments

——— Elected

- - - - Appointed by governor

LEGISLATIVE BRANCH

Senate

House of Representatives

JUDICIAL BRANCH

Supreme Court

Court of Appeals

District Courts

67 senators. Each senator serves for four years. There are 134 members of the house of representatives. Each representative serves for two years. Minnesotans elect the members of the state legislature.

JUDICIAL BRANCH

The judicial branch determines the meaning of laws. This responsibility is handled through the court system, where disputes or disagreements between parties are heard. There are two types of court cases: civil and criminal. Civil cases are disputes between citizens or other parties. They range from neighbors squabbling over loud music to someone falling and breaking a leg while on your property. Criminal offenses are those involving a crime such as robbery or murder.

Many cases begin in trial courts, which cover ten judicial districts. Three or more judges serve in each district. It is within these courts that traffic offenses and other minor disputes are handled.

The next highest court is the court of appeals. Sixteen judges preside over this court. Each judge is elected to serve for six years. If someone is not satisfied with the outcome of their case in trial court, they may request an appeal, which means that the case is reviewed by a higher court to determine if the ruling was fair. The appeals process begins in the lower courts and sometimes makes its way to the state supreme court.

Minnesota's highest (most important) court is the state supreme court. The supreme court is often called the "court of last resort" because it is the last opportunity for a case to be heard. The supreme court can overturn (reverse) the decision of a lower court, or let it remain as is. Seven judges, or justices, serve on the bench for six years.

TAKE A TOUR OF SAINT PAUL, THE STATE CAPITAL

St. Paul was developed near the banks of the mighty Mississippi, across the river from its sister city, Minneapolis. Though they are referred to as "the Twin Cities," St. Paul looks vastly different from Minneapolis. Unlike the modern steel and glass high-rise buildings that pierce the skies of downtown Minneapolis, St. Paul's skyline has the look of an earlier time. St. Paul's Cathedral and the capitol building are the tallest

St. Paul is known for its beautiful architecture and small-town charm.

47

The Minnesota History Center is home to historic artifacts and exhibits about Minnesota.

structures in the city. The capitol is nestled on a hill and offers great views of the city below.

The capitol building was completed in 1905. Twenty-two types of European marble, native limestone, sandstone, and granite went into its construction. It also has one of the largest domes in the world.

At the base of the capitol dome is a golden statue— a four-horse driven chariot, which looks down on the stairway to the entrance of the building. Inside, paintings, sculptures, and carvings feature things important to the state, such as the pink and white lady slipper and the common loon, both state symbols. Tours of the legislative chambers offer a closer look at where lawmaking begins.

Just south of the capitol grounds is the Minnesota History Center. There you can explore Minnesota up close through interactive exhibits. Climb aboard a grain elevator, listen to stories about Minnesota's pioneer days, and see nineteenth-century Minnesota as captured through the lenses of twelve photographers.

For more hands-on fun, stop at the Science Museum of Minnesota and put on a pair of 3-D glasses. Through the glasses you'll watch a laser show covering topics such as ocean exploration and flight. Then, navigate a towboat down the Mississippi River in a virtual reality exhibit.

For some quiet relaxation, take a short walk to the center of downtown St. Paul. There you'll find Town Square Park, one of the largest

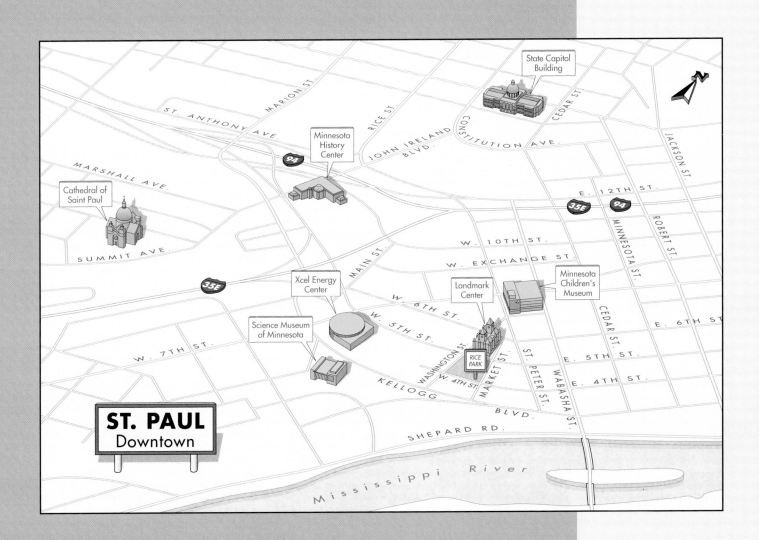

State Capitol
Building

Minnesota
History
Center

94

Cathedral of
Saint Paul

MARSHALL AVE.

MARION ST.

ST. ANTHONY AVE.

RICE ST.

JOHN IRELAND BLVD.

CONSTITUTION AVE.

CEDAR ST.

JACKSON ST.

E. 12TH ST.

35E

94

SUMMIT AVE.

MINNESOTA ST.

ROBERT ST.

W. 10TH ST.

MAIN ST.

W. EXCHANGE ST.

Minnesota
Children's
Museum

35E

Xcel Energy
Center

Landmark
Center

W. 6TH ST.

CEDAR ST.

E. 6TH ST.

W. 5TH ST.

Science Museum
of Minnesota

RICE
PARK

ST. PETER ST.

WABASHA ST.

E. 5TH ST.

W. 7TH ST.

WASHINGTON ST.

MARKET ST.

E. 4TH ST.

KELLOGG

W. 4TH ST.

BLVD.

ST. PAUL
Downtown

SHEPARD RD.

Mississippi River

indoor parks in the world. You can sit among cascading waterfalls, artificial streams, and tropical plants.

A fun way to see Minneapolis-St. Paul is by riverboat. Many local boating companies offer scenic tours along the river, from St. Paul to historic Fort Snelling, the frontier settlement built by United States army troops in the 1820s.

Costumed guides at Fort Snelling conduct tours, make crafts, and practice military drills.

CHAPTER FIVE

THE PEOPLE AND PLACES OF MINNESOTA

Minnesota is truly an "international" state. Immigrants from countries such as Great Britain, Scotland, Ireland, Denmark, Sweden, Finland, Poland, France, Italy, Germany, Russia, Korea, Vietnam, Ethiopia, and Mexico live in Minnesota and proudly celebrate their native heritages.

The largest multiethnic event in the state, The Festival of Nations, is held each April. Visitors can sample food, crafts, and music from various ethnic groups that call Minnesota home. The Scottish Country Fair, held in May, celebrates everything Scottish. The sound of bagpipes fills the air; highland dancers show off their steps, and trained border collies demonstrate shepherding. The highlight of the fair is a colorful parade.

At the Ironworld Discovery Center in Chisholm, several cultural fairs take place throughout spring and summer. Highlights include the National Polkafest, a four-day event of Polka dance and music; the

A Native American dancer performs at the annual AIM powwow at Fort Snelling State Park.

51

Slavic Celebration, a weekend of traditional music, dance, food, and craft demonstrations; and the Festival Finlandia, where ethnic food, music, and artwork are featured.

MEET THE PEOPLE

According to the 2000 census, 4,919,479 people live in the North Star State, ranking it twenty-first in population of all the states. Almost 9 in 10 Minnesotans are of European descent, 4 in every 100 are African-American, and 3 in every 100 are Latino or Hispanic. Though Native Americans once heavily inhabited the state, they now make up only 1 in every 100 people in Minnesota.

Many Minnesotans are of German and Scandinavian descent. In the early 1900s, thousands of people from Finland (part of Scandinavia) came to Minnesota to take mining jobs or to farm the land. Today, more Finnish people live in Minnesota than any other state except Michigan.

A recent surge of Asian immigrants has brought new Minnesotans from countries such as Vietnam, Cambodia, and Laos. Asians now

account for almost 3 in every 100 people. Hill people from Laos, called the Hmong, are some of America's most recent immigrants. Of the approximately 250,000 Hmong in the United States, about 60,000 live in Minnesota.

Members of an entirely different culture live in Harmony, a small farm town in southeastern Minnesota. Harmony contains the largest settlement of Amish people in the Midwest. A Mennonite religious sect, the Amish prefer more traditional ways of living. Sometimes called the plain people, the Amish grow and cook their food, build their homes and barns, and make their

The Amish work their farms with a horse and plow instead of tractors.

clothes. They farm using horse-drawn plows the way their ancestors did. They don't use electricity or drive cars. If you visit Harmony you will see many horse-drawn buggies on the roads. About one hundred Amish families live in southeastern Minnesota.

Native Americans were the original residents of Minnesota. Although they now make up less than one percent of the state's population, they have a long and rich history there. The Dakota and Ojibwe once occupied large areas of the state; now most reside on reservations. There are seven Ojibwe reservations, most of which are in northern Minnesota. The Dakota live in four communities, all located in the southern third of the state.

Taconite is mined in Fairchild, as well as other places.

WORKING IN MINNESOTA

Since the discovery of iron ore in the Mesabi, Vermilion, and Cuyuna Ranges in the late 1800s, mining has been a profitable industry and an important part of the state's economy. Today, Minnesota is still the top iron-ore producer in America. Hibbing is the site of the world's largest open-pit iron ore mine, called the Hull Rust-Mahoning Mine. More than 1.4 billion tons of earth have been removed from the ground, forming a huge, man-made canyon. Also, hundreds of ships

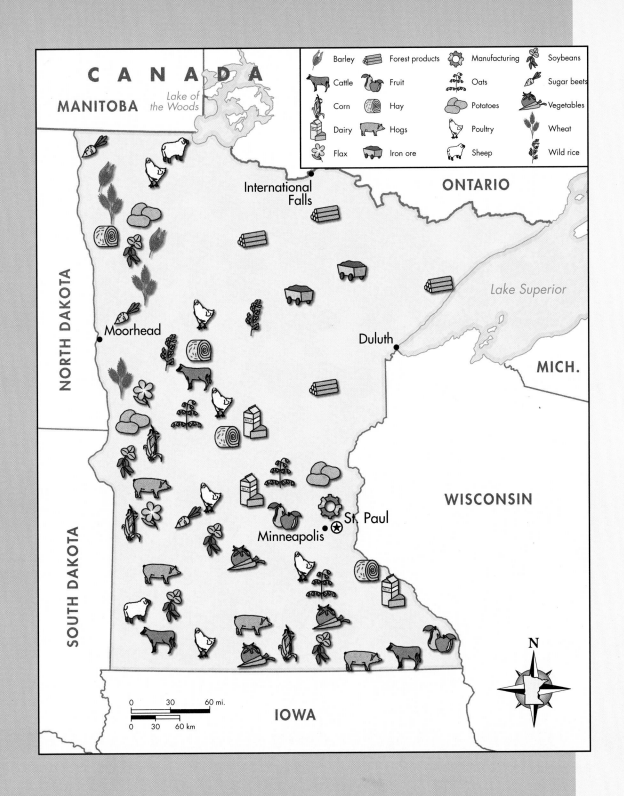

CANADA

MANITOBA

Lake of the Woods

	Barley		Forest products		Manufacturing		Soybeans
	Cattle		Fruit		Oats		Sugar beets
	Corn		Hay		Potatoes		Vegetables
	Dairy		Hogs		Poultry		Wheat
	Flax		Iron ore		Sheep		Wild rice

ONTARIO

International Falls

Lake Superior

NORTH DAKOTA

Moorhead

Duluth

MICH.

WISCONSIN

SOUTH DAKOTA

St. Paul

Minneapolis

0	30	60 mi.
0	30	60 km

IOWA

N

transport millions of tons of taconite annually from Duluth's harbor. Taconite, a flintlike rock, contains iron, making it a valuable natural resource.

Lumbering and wood manufacturing are the second-largest industries in Minnesota. Nearly 60,000 people are employed in the business. However, the state's forestry department keeps careful watch over Minnesota's timber resources. Companies must replant wherever they cut down trees. As a result, Minnesota has more trees today than it had in 1900. The wood manufacturing industry creates products such as hockey sticks, baseball bats, bird feeders, furniture, toothpicks, and paper goods.

Computer, electronic, and medical equipment companies began arriving in cities such as Minneapolis and St. Paul in the 1980s. The state is home to 3,400 electronics firms, including IBM, Honeywell, and Unisys. Retail businesses, including Marshall Fields and SuperValu, are also established there. Printing and publishing companies are the second largest manufacturing employers in the state, employing 55,000 Minnesotans.

Minnesota is one of the country's top producers of canned and frozen vegetables, flour, breakfast cereals, and rice. It is the largest sugar-beet producer in the country and ranks fifth in the production of corn, soybeans, dairy products, and hogs. It also has a very successful poultry industry. Many food-manufacturing giants are headquartered in Minnesota, including General Mills, whose most popular brands include Cheerios®, Green Giant®, and Old El Paso®.

Wild blueberries are found in some parts of Minnesota, especially in the bogs and hillsides in the northeastern part of the state. Follow this recipe to make a tasty dessert that will serve ten to twelve people. Remember to ask an adult for help!

MINNESOTA BLUEBERRY TIRAMISU

1 3-oz. package cream cheese, softened
1 cup ricotta cheese (1/2 of a 15-oz. carton)
1/3 cup frozen orange juice concentrate, thawed
1 15-3/4- or 17-1/2-oz. can vanilla or lemon
   pudding
2 3-oz. packages ladyfingers, split
3 cups blueberries
1 cup raspberries
Reddi-wip® whipped cream

1. Combine cream cheese, ricotta cheese, and orange juice concentrate in mixing bowl.
2. Add pudding, stirring until smooth.
3. Arrange half of the ladyfingers, cut-side up, in 2-quart rectangular baking dish.
4. Spoon half of the pudding mixture evenly on top.
5. Sprinkle with half of the blueberries and raspberries.
6. Repeat layers.
7. Cover and chill at least four hours, or overnight.
8. To serve, cut into pieces; garnish with Reddi-wip®.

Tourism is an important industry in Minnesota. More than 170,000 residents serve millions of visitors each year. The Mall of America in Bloomington, for example, draws 40 million people per year. It is an enormous multilevel shopping center of 4.2 million square feet (390,193 sq m), with more than 500 shops, a theme park, an aquarium, an indoor motor speedway, bowling lanes, restaurants, and fourteen movie screens.

Because of Minnesota's many parks, rivers, lakes, and rugged wilderness areas, it is the perfect nature lover's vacation. Many tourists come to the state to take advantage of the numerous hiking trails, fishing spots, water activities, and campgrounds. Let's take a tour of the state and see what it has to offer.

The Mall of America is one of the most visited places in the United States and employs about 11,000 people.

TAKE A TOUR OF MINNESOTA

Because we've already visited the state capital, you may want to start by seeing what its "twin," Minneapolis, has to offer. The Minneapolis Institute of Arts is the largest museum in the state. More than 100,000 objects spanning 5,000 years are on display.

Downtown is the Walker Art Center and Minneapolis Sculpture Garden. The Walker Art Center is best known for its twentieth-century art exhibits, its presentation of new styles of music, dance, theater, film, and video, and its innovative education programs. The Center also features an outdoor sculpture garden. One of the garden's most famous pieces is a gigantic cherry balanced on the end of an enormous spoon.

The famous Spoonbridge and Cherry sculpture was created by Claes Oldenburg and Coosje van Bruggen.

Treat yourself to a stage performance at one of the city's many theaters. The Guthrie Theater, housed in the same building as the Walker Art Center, has earned an international reputation. At the magnificent Children's Theater Company, located at the Minneapolis Institute of Arts, young actors have a chance to perform in plays such as *Cinderella*.

Minnesotans are avid sports fans, and Minneapolis is home to three professional teams: the Vikings football team, the Twins baseball team, and the Timberwolves basketball team. The Vikings and Twins play in the Hubert H. Humphrey Metrodome; the Timberwolves play home games at the Target Center.

Although Minnesota does not have a National Hockey League team, ice hockey is still a huge sport. The University of Minnesota-Duluth (UMD) men's and women's hockey teams provide exciting action for fans throughout the state. NHL Detroit Red Wing Stanley Cup Champion and 2002 Team USA Olympic Silver medalist Brett Hull played with the UMD Bulldogs before turning pro in 1985.

Basketball fans root for the Minnesota Timberwolves.

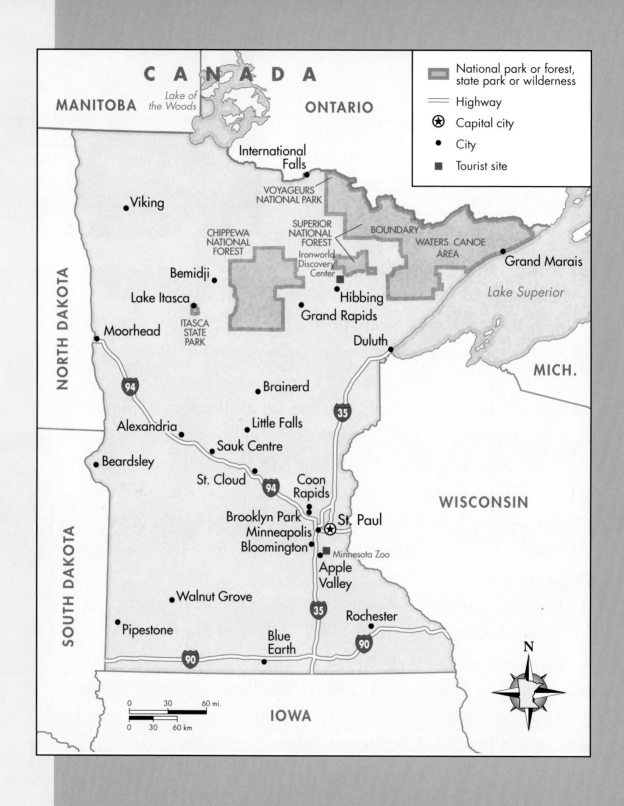

National park or forest, state park or wilderness
Highway
Capital city
City
Tourist site

CANADA

MANITOBA

Lake of the Woods

ONTARIO

International Falls

VOYAGEURS NATIONAL PARK

Viking

CHIPPEWA NATIONAL FOREST

SUPERIOR NATIONAL FOREST

BOUNDARY WATERS CANOE AREA

Grand Marais

NORTH DAKOTA

Bemidji

Lake Itasca

Ironworld Discovery Center

Hibbing

Lake Superior

Moorhead

ITASCA STATE PARK

Grand Rapids

Duluth

MICH.

94

Brainerd

35

Alexandria

Little Falls

Sauk Centre

Beardsley

St. Cloud

94

Coon Rapids

WISCONSIN

Brooklyn Park
Minneapolis
Bloomington

St. Paul

Minnesota Zoo

SOUTH DAKOTA

Apple Valley

Walnut Grove

35

Rochester

Pipestone

Blue Earth

90

90

N

0   30   60 mi.

0   30   60 km

IOWA

Women's hockey is also very popular. The UMD women's Bulldogs sent six players to the 2002 Winter Olympics in Salt Lake City, Utah. Jenny Potter, playing for the USA team, won a silver medal, while her Bulldog teammates Erika Holst and Maria Rooth won the bronze playing for the Swedish team.

Taking a walk around the city is a pleasant experience due to the city's glass-enclosed walkway system, the Skyway. Built one story above the ground, the Skyway is 52 city blocks long, or almost 5 miles (8 km). It connects shops, restaurants, offices, and apartments. The Nicollet Mall in downtown Minneapolis includes heated sidewalks for winter shoppers and plays classical music in bus shelters.

Skyways provide protection from cold winter weather and offer easy access to many shops and businesses.

Tigers at the Minnesota Zoo wander through a recreation of their natural habitat.

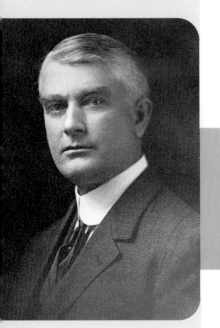

Southern Minnesota

South of the Twin Cities is nearby Apple Valley, where you can see more than 2,300 animals at the Minnesota Zoo. They are housed in exhibits that resemble natural settings, such as a rain forest and a coral reef. The zoo also features an interactive animal lab and a marine center with a shark reef and a dolphin pool.

Southeast of Apple Valley is Rochester, the largest city in the region and the fifth largest in the state, with a population of 85,806. Rochester is home to the renowned Mayo Clinic. In 1950, two of its doctors were awarded the Nobel Prize in medicine. People from around the world seek out the Mayo Clinic for medical treatment.

Southwest of Rochester is a community called Blue Earth, which earned its name from the unusual blue tint of the soil. The Green Giant packing plant harvests and processes produce there. Near the

WHO'S WHO IN MINNESOTA?

William J. Mayo (1861– 1939), together with his father and brother Charles, built the first general hospital in southeastern Minnesota in 1889. The hospital, called the Mayo Clinic, is now known around the world for its high standard of patient care.

Sioux pipe carver Ray Redwing works on a project in Pipestone.

border with South Dakota is Pipestone, where ancient Dakotas mined the red pipestone, commonly known as catlinite, that gives the town its name. Dakota descendants are still the only people permitted to extract pipestone from the town's quarries. You can purchase beautiful hand-crafted jewelry, figurines, and other pieces there.

Nearby is the tiny community of Walnut Grove, home of author Laura Ingalls Wilder. She wrote a best-selling series of children's books (the *Little House* books) based on her experiences in the midwest in the late 1800s. The Laura Ingalls Wilder Museum houses a collection of memorabilia relevant to the life of Laura and the Wilder family.

Central Minnesota

At Minnesota's "waist" is the town of Alexandria. Although fewer than 9,000 people live there, it is a popular resort for boaters and fishers because of its more than 400 lakes. In winter it is crowded with skiers, snowmobilers, and ice-fishing enthusiasts. If you'd rather stay indoors, you can visit the Runestone Museum, which houses the legendary Kensington Runestone. This 202-pound (92-kilogram) stone tablet was discovered in 1898 on a nearby farm. Some people believe that its carvings tell of a tragic Viking journey to North America in the fourteenth century.

East of Alexandria is Little Falls, named after the waterfall that supplied power to early lumber, flour, and paper mills. It is the childhood home of renowned aviator Charles Lindbergh. Today it is a center for boat building and papermaking.

In nearby Sauk Centre you can visit the boyhood home of author Sinclair Lewis. In 1930, Lewis became the first American to win the Nobel Prize for literature, and many of his novels were set in Sauk Centre. Sauk Centre is also the basis for author Garrison Keillor's imaginary town, Lake Wobegon.

The west central part of Minnesota is sometimes called Vikingland because many immigrants from Northern Europe settled there in the late nineteenth century. In Moorhead you can view a replica of a Viking longship, built by schoolteacher Robert Asp. In 1982, the ship sailed from Duluth to Bergen, Norway—a trip of 6,352 miles (10,223 km).

You can step across the Mississippi River without getting your feet wet if you walk across the rocks at Lake Itasca, where the mighty river's

Tourists walk across the headwaters of the Mississippi River at Lake Itasca.

headwaters (beginnings) are found. Vacationers also flock to the vast Itasca State Park, spanning 32,000 acres (12,950 ha). Near Lake Itasca is Bemidji, home of the legendary giant Paul Bunyan. Tall tales say that the huge lumberjack and his blue ox, Babe, were once the most powerful logging team in the North.

North Central Minnesota

Sharing its border with Ontario, Canada, is the state's only national park, called Voyageurs. Named for the French-Canadian explorers who navigated the waters in search of furs and other trading goods, the 218,000-acre (88,222-ha) park is a maze of small islands, lakes, and forested areas. One third of the park is water, so the best way to get around is by boat. When the waters freeze over in the winter months, the park is visited by snowmobilers, cross-country skiers, and ice fisherman.

The Voyageurs forest areas are also home to many wild animals including timberwolves, bears, moose, deer, and lynx. There are also plenty of hiking trails and camping sites. At Voyageurs you can take a canoe excursion on Kabetogama Lake, or hike the 9-mile (14-km) Cruiser Lake Trail where you may spot a moose, heron, or loon.

Northeastern Minnesota

Duluth is the fourth largest city in the state. Situated at the southwestern tip of Lake Superior, it has been a major commercial center since its founding in the mid 1800s. Forty million tons of cargo pass through Duluth's port annually. Grain elevators, ore landings, and shipyards line its 47 miles (76 km) of docks.

Duluth is one of the busiest ports in the nation, as well as one of the leading ports on the Great Lakes.

The harbor is shielded by a long spit of land called Minnesota Point. Connecting the two is the 386-foot (118-m) Aerial Lift Bridge. Canal Park, on the Duluth Ship Canal, features shops, a boardwalk, and an indoor amusement park with batting cages, basketball courts, and a video arcade.

In the city, visitors can take in a concert or see the ballet at the Duluth Entertainment Convention Center. North Shore Drive, which follows the shore of Lake Superior and reaches to Thunder Bay, Ontario, offers a beautiful view of the lake and has places for water sports, camping, hiking, cross-country skiing, and snowmobiling.

Other attractions in the northeastern part of the state include Boundary Waters Canoe Area Wilderness, where you can paddle your way along 1,200 miles (1,931 km) of canoe routes. Not far from there is Ironworld Discovery Center, where the history of the pioneer mining days is recreated through interactive exhibits.

It is easy to see how Minnesota earned the nickname the North Star State. With its historical, natural, and cultural wealth, Minnesota truly is a star among states.

The Boundary Waters
Canoe Area Wilderness
has about 1,200 miles
(1,931 km) of canoe routes.

MINNESOTA ALMANAC

Statehood date and number: May 11, 1858; 32nd

State seal: A barefoot farmer plowing a field near the Falls of St. Anthony. The farmer's gun, axe, and powderhorn are leaning on a tree stump. Behind the farmer, a Native American on horseback is riding toward the setting sun. Above them is the state motto, *L'etoile du Nord* (The Star of the North). Adopted 1861.

State flag: The flag is royal blue, bordered in gold fringe. The original seal design is on the flag. The seal is surrounded by a wreath of lady slippers, the state flower. Around the wreath is a ring of 19 stars. The largest star represents Minnesota, the 19th state after the original thirteen to enter the Union. Adopted 1957.

Geographic center: Crow Wing, 10 miles (16 km) southwest of Brainerd

Total area/rank: 86,943 square miles (225,181 sq km)/12th

Borders: Canadian provinces of Manitoba and Ontario; Wisconsin, Lake Superior, North Dakota, South Dakota, Iowa

Latitude and longitude: Minnesota is located approximately between 43° 30' and 49° 23' N and 89° 29' and 97° 13' W.

Highest/lowest elevation: Eagle Mountain in Cook County, 2,301 feet (701 m)/along Lake Superior, 602 feet (183 m)

Hottest/coldest temperature: 114° F (46° C); recorded twice: in Beardsley on July 29, 1917 and in Moorhead on July 6, 1936/–60° F (–51° C) in Tower on February 2, 1996

Total land area/rank: 79,617 square miles (206,207 square km)/14th

Inland water area/rank: 4,780 square miles (12,380 sq km), excluding 2,546 square miles (6,594 sq km) of Lake Superior

Population (2000 census)/rank: 4,919,479/ 21st

Population of major cities:

Minneapolis: 382,618

St. Paul: 287,151

Duluth: 86,918

Rochester: 85,806

Bloomington: 85,172

Origin of state name: From the Dakota word *minisota*, meaning "sky-tinted water"

State capital: St. Paul (established 1849)

Counties: 87

State government: 67 senators, 134 representatives

Major rivers/lakes: Blue Earth, Cannon, Crow Wing, Little Fork, Middle, Minnesota, Mississippi, Red, Pomme de Terre, Rapid, Red Lake, Redwood, St. Croix, St. Louis, Thief/Big Sandy, Bowstring, Kabetogama, Lake of the Woods, Leech, Lower Red, Red Lake, Mille Lacs, Minnetonka, Otter Tail, Pepin, Superior, Winnibigoshish

Farm products: Apples, barley, blueberries, butter, carrots, cheese, corn, green peas, hay, milk, oats, onions, potatoes, rye, soybeans, strawberries, sugar beets, sunflowers, wheat, wild rice

Livestock: Poultry, cattle, hogs, sheep

Manufactured products: Canned foods, cereals, chemicals, computers and computer equipment, farm and construction machinery, flour, paper products, printed materials, scientific and medical instruments

Mining products: Granite, gravel, iron ore, limestone, peat, sandstone, taconite

Bird: Common loon (*Gavia immer*), adopted 1961

Drink: Milk, adopted 1984

Fish: Walleye (*Stizostedion vitreum*), adopted 1965

Flower: Pink and white lady slipper (*Cypripedium reginae*), adopted 1902

Gem: Lake Superior Agate, adopted 1969

Grain: Wild rice (*Zizania aquatica*), adopted 1977

Motto: *L'Etoile du Nord* (The Star of the North)

Muffin: Blueberry

Mushroom: Morel (*Morchella esculenta*), adopted 1984

Nicknames: North Star State; Gopher State; Land of 10,000 Lakes

Song: "Hail, Minnesota" (by Truman E. Rickard and Arthur E. Upson), adopted 1945

Tree: Norway Pine (*pinus resinosa*), adopted 1953

Wildlife: American toad, Blandings turtle, four-toed salamander, gopher snake, gray treefrog, massassagua, northern cricket frog, snapping turtle, timber rattlesnake, Baird's sparrow, bald eagle, blackbird, burrowing owl, duck, loon, meadowlark, owl, peregrine falcon, pheasant, piping plover, sparrow, woodpecker, wren, bass, brook and rainbow trout, blue catfish, bluegill, bullhead, carp, coho and chinook salmon, crappie, lake herring, Lake Superior cisco, largemouth and smallmouth bass, muskellunge (muskies), northern pike, rock sturgeon, smelt, sunfish, walleye, whitefish, yellow perch, badger, beaver, black bear, bobcat, gopher, gray wolf (endangered), mink, moose, muskrat, opossum, otter, porcupine, raccoon, red fox, skunk, timberwolf, white-tailed deer

TIMELINE

MINNESOTA STATE HISTORY

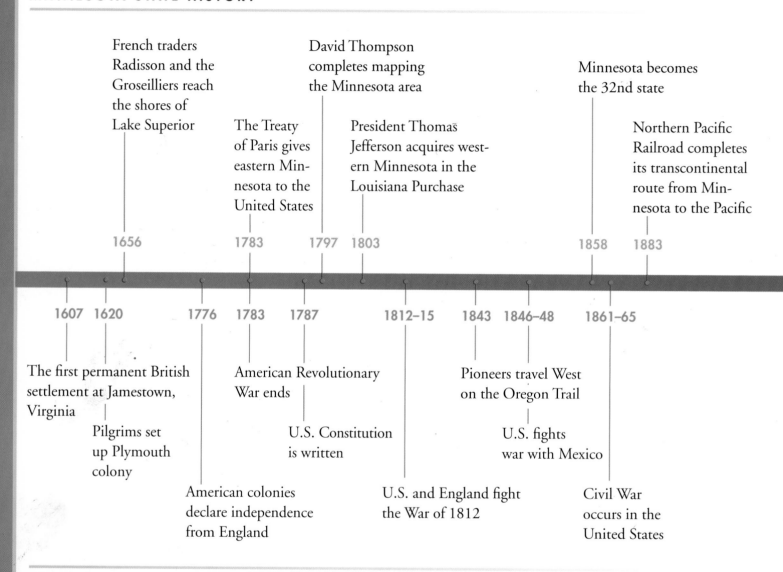

French traders Radisson and the Groseilliers reach the shores of Lake Superior

The Treaty of Paris gives eastern Minnesota to the United States

David Thompson completes mapping the Minnesota area

President Thomas Jefferson acquires western Minnesota in the Louisiana Purchase

Minnesota becomes the 32nd state

Northern Pacific Railroad completes its transcontinental route from Minnesota to the Pacific

1656   1783   1797   1803   1858   1883

1607   1620   1776   1783   1787   1812–15   1843   1846–48   1861–65

The first permanent British settlement at Jamestown, Virginia

Pilgrims set up Plymouth colony

American Revolutionary War ends

American colonies declare independence from England

U.S. Constitution is written

U.S. and England fight the War of 1812

Pioneers travel West on the Oregon Trail

U.S. fights war with Mexico

Civil War occurs in the United States

UNITED STATES HISTORY

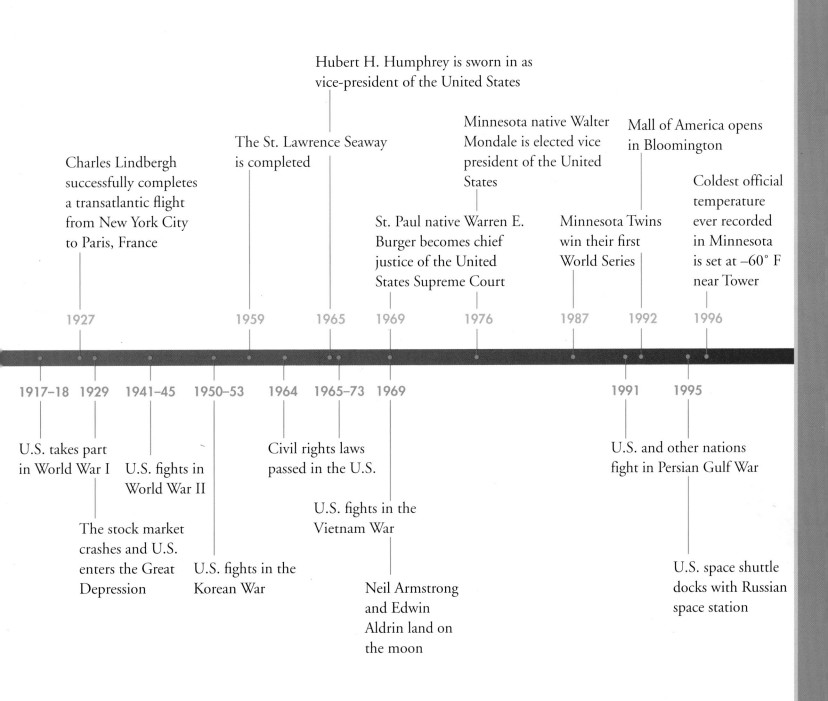

Hubert H. Humphrey is sworn in as vice-president of the United States

The St. Lawrence Seaway is completed

Minnesota native Walter Mondale is elected vice president of the United States

Mall of America opens in Bloomington

Charles Lindbergh successfully completes a transatlantic flight from New York City to Paris, France

Coldest official temperature ever recorded in Minnesota is set at –60° F near Tower

St. Paul native Warren E. Burger becomes chief justice of the United States Supreme Court

Minnesota Twins win their first World Series

1927   1959   1965   1969   1976   1987   1992   1996

1917–18 1929 1941–45 1950–53 1964 1965–73 1969   1991   1995

U.S. takes part in World War I

U.S. fights in World War II

Civil rights laws passed in the U.S.

U.S. and other nations fight in Persian Gulf War

The stock market crashes and U.S. enters the Great Depression

U.S. fights in the Korean War

U.S. fights in the Vietnam War

Neil Armstrong and Edwin Aldrin land on the moon

U.S. space shuttle docks with Russian space station

GALLERY OF FAMOUS MINNESOTANS

Louie Anderson

(1953–)

Stand-up comedian and actor. Creator of multiple award-winning animated series *Life with Louie*. Born in Minneapolis.

Richard Dean Anderson

(1950–)

Actor best known for his role in the television series *MacGyver*. Born in Minneapolis.

Bob Dylan

(1941–)

Influential singer/songwriter of the 1960s and 1970s. Born in Duluth and grew up in Hibbing.

Mary GrandPré

(1954–)

Illustrator of the American Harry Potter books. Lives in Minneapolis.

Garrison Keillor

(1942–)

Host of the well-known Minnesota Public Radio show *A Prairie Home Companion*. Born in Anoka.

Jessica Lange

(1949–)

Two-time Academy Award winning actress for her roles in *Tootsie* and *Blue Sky*. Born in Cloquet.

Walter Mondale

(1928–)

Served as vice president of the United States from 1977 to 1981. Made unsuccessful bid for the presidency in 1984. Born in Ceylon.

Prince

(1958–)

Born Prince Rogers Nelson, a multitalented award-winning composer, director, and musician. Born in Minneapolis.

Charles Schulz

(1922–2000)

Cartoonist who created Snoopy, Charlie Brown, Lucy, Linus, and other characters portrayed in the famous syndicated cartoon strip *Peanuts*. Born in St. Paul.

Dave Winfield

(1951–)

Major league baseball player who was awarded seven Golden Glove awards. Finished his major league baseball career with a lifetime batting average of .283, with more than 3,000 hits and 465 home runs. Born in St. Paul.

GLOSSARY

amendment: change in an existing law or constitution

amphibian: cold-blooded vertebrate that lives on land and in water

archaeologist: scientist who studies material remains, such as relics and artifacts, of past civilizations

constitution: fundamental rules or laws for the government of a city or nation

controversy: a prolonged dispute or argument

cooperative: association owned by and operated for the benefit of its members who use its services

drift: a mixture of various soils and stone deposited by a glacier

geologist: scientist who studies the Earth, including its physical structure and history

missionary: person sent to spread a religious faith or to engage in charitable work with religious support

multilingual: the ability to speak and understand more than one language

nomad: a tribe or community of people who move from one place to another to survive

petroglyph: image that is scratched or carved into a cliff, boulder, or any type of rock

precipitation: rain, sleet, ice, or snow

siege: the placing of an army around a fortified place to capture it; a continued attack

transatlantic: crossing or extending across the Atlantic Ocean

urban: relating to a city or town

FOR MORE INFORMATION

Websites

The Minnesota Page

http://deckernet.com/minn/
A collection of web pages about and for the North Star state.

Minnesota Historical Society

http://www.mnhs.org/
Information about Minnesota past and present.

Minnesota Office of Tourism

http://www.exploreminnesota.com
Minnesota travel and vacation website.

The Dakota Society

http://www.visi.com/~vanmulken/welcome.htm
Information about the history and culture of Native Americans.

Minnesota Secretary of State Student Page

http://www.sos.state.mn.us/student/history.html
Important documents and maps pertaining to Minnesota, and links to relevant websites.

Books

Butler, Dori Hillestad. *M Is for Minnesota.* Minnesota: University of Minnesota Press, 1998.

Carlson, Jeffrey D. *A Historical Album of Minnesota.* Brookfield, CT: Millbrook Press, 1993.

Greenberg, Keith Elliot. *Jesse Ventura.* Minneapolis, MN: Lerner Publications, 1999.

Marsh, Carole. *Minnesota Government for Kids.* Peachtree City, GA: Gallopade International, 1996.

O'Hara, Megan. *Frontier Fort: Fort Life on the Upper Mississippi, 1826.* Mankato, MN: Capstone Press, 1998.

Rambeck, Richard. *The History of the Minnesota Twins.* Mankato, MN: The Creative Company, 2000.

Addresses

Minnesota Historical Society

345 W. Kellogg Boulevard
St. Paul, MN 55102

Minnesota Travel Information Center

100 Metro Square, 121 7th Place E
St. Paul, MN 55101

Office of the Governor

130 State Capitol, 75 Constitution Avenue
St. Paul, MN 55155

INDEX

ABOUT THE AUTHOR

Judy L. Hasday, a native of Philadelphia, Pennsylvania, received her Bachelor of Arts degree in communications and an Ed.M. in instructional technologies from Temple University. An award-winning author, Hasday has written several books for young adults including *Extraordinary Women Athletes*, *The Apollo 13 Mission*, *The Holocaust*, and biographies of actor James Earl Jones and former Secretary of State Madeleine Albright. Pet Zebra finches Atticus, B. J., Isaac, Jacob, and Skye keep her company while she writes. Her hobbies include travel photography and collecting signed modern first-edition books.